The Guide To Network Marketing

By: Eric Knight Jr
©2019 By Eric Knight Jr

****

FREE DOWNLOAD

Get your free copy of the
5 Network Marketing Success
Killers mini-book.
Go to the web address below…

NmRegister.ekjbooks.com

****

TABLE OF CONTENTS

Chapter   *Page #*

Intro

The fact that you are reading this leads me to one logical conclusion....

You are working to get better at your Network Marketing business. Well I am happy to help you with that, but I have only one stipulation…you have to be honest with both yourself and with me. That is the only way this works.

If I may speak freely, most people are lying to themselves. They tell themselves things like "I am trying as hard as I can!" when honestly they aren't doing anything they should be doing.

Some people don't accept any responsibility for where their business is currently. If you are one of those people, then I can't do anything for you. In fact, if you only want to complain and can't handle the truth, then you might as well get your money back now.

You know why?

Because if you are lying to yourself and feeling like you can't change, you won't change. You can have every specific step to the life of your dreams, but those steps won't matter if you lie to yourself and make yourself believe that you can't do it.

So again, if I am going to give you the answers you have been searching for, such as how you can earn money in this industry, then right now you have to give me your word that you are going to be honest, and I will make a deal with you. I will give you my word that I will be honest with you too.

WARNING: I have been told that I am brutally honest, and I am going to give it to you raw. In fact, some of you are going to quit the industry all together after reading this book, which should save you time and money. (That was my first bit of harsh honesty in case you missed it). The truth is that some of you don't need to be in this industry, and that is ok.

It definitely isn't for everyone.

Now that we have that out of the way, let's get to it.

Is This Industry For You?

I have been in this industry for almost 20 years at the time of this writing. I have been a part of businesses consisting of wellness products, nutritional juices, long distance, telecommunications, and travel. People have approached me with actual pyramid schemes. Just to be clear, I have never participated in a scheme and would never knowingly do so. My point in all of this is to let you know that I have extensive knowledge of the industry.

If your Journey has been anything like mine, then it has been full of people telling you **how much money they have made** and showing you all of the things that they have acquired with that money. Some even show you their checks (Which is illegal by the way, It's called enticement.), and guess what...many of them are LYING.

Please understand that not everyone is lying - this industry is real, but whenever you have something real, you will also have imposters.

Experience has shown me that people who really make a lot of money don't work so hard to convince you that they are making money. I have heard talk of people renting luxury cars. I know of people who cashed their whole paycheck from their 9 to 5 and pretended that the money came from their business, and even some who made fake photocopied checks.

What you have is people faking their success. You see them and you feel like they can help you make money because they are "so successful". So you sign up with them. Then they put the word out about you joining them. Other people see that you signed up with this person who makes a lot of money, so they join too.

What ends up happening, is this person has tricked so many people that now they are actually making real money. This is the cycle.

The big problem with the cycle is that things that are built on lies eventually crumble. Why? They crumble because Network Marketing is an industry of duplication. If you are working really hard, but don't have a team that is doing the same, you just have a sales job with incentives. If you don't have duplication in this industry, you don't have anything.

The ability to get paid for helping a team of people build their businesses and achieve their dreams is what the industry is really about. Unfortunately, many people make money while the majority of the other hard workers on their team make little to nothing.

That is like someone driving a stick shift and the car is constantly jerking down the road stripping the gears in the process. You might get to your destination, but you aren't doing it right.

It is only a matter of time before things break down permanently. So it is very important to join a team that has an actual system in place that leads to real long term duplication.

The truth is that many of the people who have made a lot of money have no idea how to help YOU make money, but they still want to sign you on their team…. and they are going to tell you whatever they need to tell you to get you to sign up.

Outside of money, the next most common lie (in my experience) is **"This business is sooooo easy***!!***"**.

I am here to tell you that this is completely false. This leads people to believe that they can make money without doing any work. If you have a good team that is following a good duplicable system, then business can be SIMPLE, but run from anyone who tells you that you can easily make a lot of money. They are either lying or doing something illegal.

You will have to do plenty work, especially in the beginning, but you can do the necessary work in limited time. I am sure that you have heard it, and it is true that you can build a Network Marketing business part-time. But keep in mind that part-time could be 10 to 15 hours a week. While that isn't a lot of time it is more time than most people expect to spend after someone tells them how "easy" everything is.

Another major misconception (lie) is **"All you have to do is get on my team and you will make**

money". I don't care how efficient or simple a team's system is, you will have to do something!

A business that pays you money without doing anything is likely a SCAM. Your paying money to join isn't enough. Only Passive Income Producing Assets pay you without you having to do something more than paying money to start, and even they require a little work on the front end.

Network marketing is one of the few ways I know of where anyone of legal age has an opportunity to become rich. It doesn't matter if you have a Master's degree or if you dropped out in pre-school. It doesn't matter if you have been to jail or if you have bad credit. Everyone has the same opportunity to make more money in a month than most people make in a year working jobs.

Having said that, anything that allows you to make money is going to attract scammers and crooks. So keep your eyes open and be smart. Prayers don't hurt either.

Now let's look at the other side of that coin. Some businesses are much more difficult than they should be. Not all businesses are created equal. You need to know the differences that matter and the ones that don't.

One of the top things that people use to get others to join their team is the Compensation Plan. If I had a dollar for every time someone said "You have to see our comp-plan! We have the best comp-plan in the world!", I would not need a business or any other way to make money.

I hate to break it to those people but there are numerous good comp-plans out there. They aren't all the same, but many are good. It really depends on what you are looking for.

That said, not all plans are created equal. They do have differences. You just have to get the plan that works best for you.

Some plans are Front Heavy (aka bonus heavy), meaning the majority of your money is earned in response to doing something such as having someone purchase a start up product pack to joint the team.

Some plans are Back Heavy meaning they pay you high residual commissions.

Then there are plans that are viewed as balanced plans. These plans have good up front bonuses and good residuals. The bonuses are your right now money and the residual is your long term 'quit your job' money.

I personally believe the balanced plan is the best. Front Heavy plans seem to attract the crooks because they (the crooks) usually figure out a way to take advantage of those really big bonuses and make a lot of money...illegally.

Those companies, in my opinion, have higher turnover rates because they don't have the long term money to keep people from jumping to another business, and the Back Heavy plans make it harder for you to earn a living while you learn to build your business. It could take years for you to build up enough residual income to live on.

Without those upfront bonuses, you could really struggle financially while learning to run your business. That is why I believe that a balanced plan is the best. There are many variations of each type of the 3 plans, so you just have to choose the one that is best for you.

We have talked about many of the harsh truths of the Network Marketing Industry. If you are still interested in the industry then great. I just want to make sure that you know the truth. I firmly believe that having false expectations means sure failure for people in this industry.

If you're still interested, let's get down to business.

GETTING CUSTOMERS

This is a section that sadly won't apply to all of you because unfortunately, many of you are with companies that don't value getting customers.

Maybe you don't value getting customers either. Maybe all you care about is recruiting people into your business and getting those quick bonuses.

Maybe you don't have a product that pays much in the form of residual income. For example, those companies that pay small residuals on their products or services (such as 1% or 2%) might end up paying you literally pennies, depending on what the product is.

Long distance call companies used to be notorious for this. People rarely used long distance and they only paid about 2%.

When you coupled that with a long distance bill running $2 for the month, it equaled a residual payout that wasn't worth the time.

This is the kind of thing that keeps business people in our industry from focusing on gathering customers. However, if you run into someone who only values signing business owners and they don't care about customers, don't walk away, run!

The FTC (Federal Trade Commission) has a job of making sure that businesses are actual businesses and not schemes. If you will allow me to make a definition for the sake of our topic, a scheme is something that promises money being made without the sale of a product or service, or the purchase of an asset.

The easiest way for you to get a bad reputation is for you to get caught up in a scheme that winds up getting shut down by the FTC. A company should offer products or a service as a product. An example is a legal service.

But some services are questionable when it comes to Networking Marketing. Take travel businesses for example. It can always be argued that travel isn't a product, but the real problem in many travel companies is that the business owners don't travel, nor do they sell travel. They sell the idea of making money by having a travel business.

So here you are with a company that is selling travel as a product. The company is making good money, but there is one problem... the company isn't booking any travel.

So the FTC investigates and determines that too much of the company's income comes from signups and people paying their monthly requirements to stay active in the business, not from booking travel.

If your business doesn't have customers, you don't have a business. This is why customers are so vital. Therefore I suggest that you only align yourself with a company that values it's customers and puts emphasis on both customer acquisition and business owners... that is if you want to create that rare and mysterious walk away residual income that you always hear about.

That income only comes from "actual customers" purchasing "actual products" over and over again.

So you need to be great at getting and keeping customers. (I don't guess there is any point in going into great detail about how *quality* products would help you as it pertains to your business.) The next question is **how** do you get and keep customers?

This is going to be another section that is difficult to go into specific detail about because you all represent so many different companies, so we will go over the fundamental information that should apply to anyone.

Ok. **Step 1** is going to sound simple and that's because it is. Your first priority is to create as many testimonials as you can, as quickly as you can.

(**Step 2**) you share those testimonials with as many people as possible as quickly as you can.

One of my mentors said it best when she said *"You can't argue with testimonials!"*, and it is so true. Accumulating as many legit testimonials as quickly, (and morally), as possible will help you in multiple areas.

Someone could argue with you and tell you that your product is no good or that they aren't sure if it works, but they will sound pretty silly if you have several documented testimonials.

Creating testimonials legitimizes your product. Legitimizing your product legitimizes your business, and the more legitimate the perception of your business is, the more money you stand to make as long as you are willing to work.

So it doesn't matter if your product is coffee or water filters, you need to get that product into the hands of as many people as you can, as quickly as possible, and of course document the results.

A testimonial you can't prove is useless. So take pictures, make videos, or write them down, but document your testimonials with name, city, and state.

The next question is how do you get the products into their hands, and for that matter, who are 'they' anyways?

The truth of the matter is when you decide that you are serious about your business, you have to start with an all out blitz. You have to give it everything that you have because if you don't, it is not very likely that you will build enough momentum to keep it going.

Make no mistake, Network Marketing is an industry of momentum. Momentum is best created with speed, but it is **always** created with consistency. If you are consistent, you can build momentum slowly or quickly. I rarely use the word never, but you will never get your business to a high level if you are inconsistent.

Nothing is worse than starting and stopping. Starting and stopping is just another name for the painful and slow death of your business.

Think of it this way. When you have products or a service that you are selling, you basically have a store.

Let's face it, although many products have proprietary ingredients, there aren't very many proprietary products.

In other words, the tea that you sell might have special attributes that no other tea has, but it is still tea, and that is exactly how most potential customers see it. They feel as though they can go somewhere else and get tea or whatever your product happens to be. Guess what... in most cases they are right.

I can practically hear some of you now... "Oh no! Nothing is like our product!!". That may be true, but as far as a potential customer is concerned, they can take their money and go elsewhere.

One of the easiest ways to send your potential customers to the competition is by being inconsistent with your business.

Imagine that someone told you about a great store. You jump in the car or head online and check it out, but when you get there, it's closed during normal business hours, so you assume that something must have happened. No big deal. You go back a few days later and the store is open. Everything was just as great as you were told it would be.

You tell a friend about the store. The friend then goes to the store during the appropriate business hours and the store is closed again! About a week later, you both get together and ride to the store, but again, it is closed.

Would you continue to go to a store when you have no idea when it will be open or closed? Probably not.

That is how you look to people when you constantly start and stop. They don't trust you when you are inconsistent, and they just go somewhere else. Being consistent is crucial for repeat business. So as many of my mentors have said, *"Always be open"*. Always work your business consistently.

The only time it is ok to start and stop is when you are doing a Mental Restart. I am a huge advocate for MENTAL restarts. A 'Mental Restart' is essentially pretending that you are starting your business completely from scratch even if you are at the highest level in your company. With a 'Mental Restart', you never actually stop, so it is very different from starting and stopping.

The next thing you need to do to keep customers is "Be Professional".

People prefer to deal with professionals, especially when it comes to their money. This pretty much speaks for itself.

Being professional simply put is doing the things you say you will do, when you say you will do them, and doing them the best you can do them. I will elaborate on professionalism in just a bit, but for now, let's put a little more emphasis on getting customers and getting them quickly because you can't keep what you don't have.

Contrary to your fears and what many people say, if you want to get off to a quick start, you probably need to start with your friends and family. If the people who know you and care about you won't take action with you, you will likely have a really hard time getting someone who doesn't really know you to join you.

I specialize in getting friends and family to participate in my businesses as both customers and business owners. I have had people join the team who previously told other family members no in regards to the same business.

Was it because I made a lot of money? No. The first time it happened I was just getting started on my business journey, so my money wasn't funny...it was hilarious. There is one reason and one reason only why I can sign up those closest to me without a problem.

Correction, there are a couple of reasons. The first is that I build relationships with people, not just business relationships, but actual relationships. Relationships are vitally important because this is a people business. It is much easier to communicate with someone when you have a relationship with them.

The second reason is because I understand the importance of being professional, especially with people who know you. This is where most people drop the ball.

Let's get to another example. One of the main reasons people struggle with family and friends is because their family and friends don't respect them as business people.

Let's say that a person is a part of an opportunity that has a presentation system of a video, a party, or meeting, followed by a demonstration, but when it comes to family-people often want to freestyle.

Here is an example with a person named Tom…Tom looks at his presentation and says *"You know, the video is great, but it won't work on my uncle. You don't know my uncle."* Sound familiar?

Or how about this one *"My aunt knows all about this type of business. She has had businesses before. We don't have to do all of that for her. She just needs me to talk to her"*.

And my absolute favorite *"Mom, I started a business and I need you to sign up."*

These examples are what many business people do when it comes to friends and family. These are also some of the most unprofessional strategies you could use. Imagine walking into a department store and the sales person didn't tell you anything about a product, but just said "Hey, I'm new here and I really need you to buy this." You would think they were too incompetent to have their job.

That tactic is just as ineffective when you use it. You not only need to be professional with friends and family, but you need to be more professional with them than with anyone else.

"Why" you ask?
My theory is that many people have misconceptions about other people. Those misconceptions could be based on race, sex, age, financial status, or any number of things. The

people who are closest to you can share those misconceptions about you as well, but even if they don't have the aforementioned misconceptions, many of the people closest to you will have one of the strongest misconceptions of all... the misconception that they know what you are capable of, and they base this on your past and what they think they know about you currently.

Sometimes those closest to you feel like they know you too well to take you seriously. So you have to be so professional that they forget that you are 'you'. This doesn't mean that you have to be someone you aren't, but you do have to be professional.

What is being professional? Being

professional in a nutshell is don't do (or not do) anything that you wouldn't do if you had to meet with someone who is really important... specifically things like: being late, being late without calling to let someone know that you are running behind, being dressed inappropriately, or begging.

If your family sees you as sloppy, always late, irresponsible, and needy outside of business, unless you give them a side of you they have never seen, that is exactly how they will see you in business. In other words, they don't respect you. How do you get respect? By earning it. You earn it by showing people that even if everything that I listed above is true about you, none of it applies to you when it comes to business.

Real business pros don't expect something for nothing. A pro doesn't expect a family member or friend to do it simply because we are family or friends. You go to family or friends dressed appropriately for your business and you give them the most solid version of your presentation. Don't come up with something "new and special", just give them the best version of your normal presentation.

Also remember, Network Marketing is an industry of duplication, so always keep in mind that whenever you do a presentation or anything as it regards to your business, you are showing the other person what they will have to do if they decide to join you. So keep it professional, and keep it simple.

The fastest way for you to get customers (this includes friends and family) is for you to contact as many people as possible. So the first thing you need to do is start your list. Get some paper and number it 1 through at least 150. (You could do this on a computer as well, but there is something about writing your list out by hand). I can already hear some of you crying "I don't know that many people!". If you are over 18, you know 150 other people who are at least 18 years old.

The major requirement for your list is that everyone on it must be someone you can contact. It does you no good to list your best friend from the 9th grade if you have no idea where she is nor do you have a way to find her. Therefore, the best place to start your list of family and friends is your cell phone.

But keep in mind that "someone you can get in touch with" doesn't necessarily mean that you have to have their phone number. If you put your next door neighbor on the list, but you don't have her phone number, it is ok because you can always go next door and talk to her.

The next best place is social media. Social media allows you to contact anyone who is your friend, and depending on the social media platform, you might be able to contact people who aren't your friend (Many of you probably already have around a thousand friends.). Put them on your list.

Finally, you can use a memory jogger. A memory jogger is something that helps you to think of people you know who you might not think of initially, such as your dentist or the family attorney.

Once you have your list, it's time to make some calls. That's right. You have to talk to people.

Finally, don't underestimate the importance of keeping your customers. Tell people thank you, and send them cards for ordering from you for 3 consecutive months. Send out a hand written letter thanking your customers. Don't take people for granted.

It is much easier to keep a customer than it is to get a new customer, so make sure that you show your customers that you appreciate them, and then you can focus on **getting** customers instead of **REPLACING** customers.

WHY YOU NEED A COACH

One of the biggest misconceptions about the Network Marketing Industry is that anyone can do it...alone.

Now when I say alone, I am not talking about your team, I am talking about your mentor or coach. I am talking about you thinking that you can build this type of business with no guidance or development.

Well I am here to help. Consider me your honorary coach.

When I started in this industry, it was way too hard to find someone who could tell me what I needed to do to be successful. That is why I wrote this guide.

You might be wondering what qualifies me to be a coach? I am glad you asked.

Here is a **tip**. When you are looking for someone to give you guidance and help you to accomplish your goals, you don't go by the amount of success that that person has had as an individual. You need to find out how their team is doing.

When you join someone's team, you are not going to be "that actual person", you are going to be _another person on their team_. So it shouldn't matter to you how much money the individual you signed up with has made or what kind of car they drive. They could have earned those things with attributes that they have, but can't give you.

What you need to ask is....

"How is your team doing?".

-How many people <u>on their team</u> are making the kind of money that they are talking to you about?

-How many are making any money at all?

-How many people do you have who have never made money in this industry before?

-How many did you directly work with and help to become successful?

These are the questions that you need to be asking someone who tells you about the money you can be making on their team.

I had multiple people qualified for a company

car on my team. I had numerous people who made money with us who had never been able to make money in business prior to joining our business team, and many who had never owned their own business before. I also had many who hit their career highs on our business team. I had a really good team (I still do).

This is the type of information you need to know before you join someone's team. That is what this guide is for...to be your coach. FYI, coaching does not replace Self Development. A good coach will make sure that you understand the importance of Self Development.

The Importance Of Self Development

I can make a very strong argument for this being the most important chapter in this book. Self-Development, utilizing motivational speakers, and believing "you are as you think", - to some are very cliché things. Perhaps that's why people tend to overlook this very important aspect of success. But if you choose one section of this guide to buy into, let this be the one.

What does Self Development mean to you? That question is something that you should really think about. In the meantime, let me tell you what it means to me.

By my own definition, *self development occurs when a person takes the necessary steps to make the transformation from the person they are now into the person they need to be to be able to accomplish their goals and fulfill their destiny*.

I would love to use the word 'Never' in this situation, but since I really don't like that word, I will just say it is very unlikely that a person with large goals will achieve those goals without going through some type of developmental change.

Let me relate it to networking. Most people don't make $60,000 a yr, ($5k a month), nor do most people own a business. So for people who make 20k to 50k a year and have never run their own business, to get to a point where they run their business well enough to make not 20k to 50k a year, but 20k to 30k a month… let's just say that they are going to have to make some major mental changes.

One thing that I really like about our industry is that like God, it is no respecter of men. No one is born with everything it takes to be successful in this industry, and someone who has never run a business needs even more training. Specifically, you need to develop mentally.

The first level of mental change (and arguably the most important) is belief. You first must believe that you can accomplish something that is new, bigger than you, and initially very uncomfortable. You have to train your mind to do business because many of the things that must be done to have a successful business are very different from what an inexperienced person would think you should do.

The most important thing that a non-business person must understand is the idea of working without being paid immediately. This doesn't mean that you will never get paid, but you sometimes have to work a while before you see profits.

You have to be mentally strong and have faith that your work will pay off if you continue to do the correct things. This is a really difficult concept for many people to embrace. As a society, we want to believe that if we do the right things, we will get positive results immediately, and if we do the wrong things, we will get negative results.

This also implies that if we get negative results, the only explanation is that we did the wrong things. That is not always the case.

Let me give you an example. Network marketing (and life in general) can be related to many things. For the sake of this example, we will relate it to fishing.

Have you ever been fishing? If you haven't you will still be able to follow, but if you have, this example will really hit home. I compare the industry to fishing because they both share the fact that you can do everything exactly right and still get negative results.

In the case of fishing, you can use the right bait, be out at the right time of day, drop bait in the perfect spot, and not catch a dang thing. (I mean not even get a nibble - like the whole lake is empty.) But you know it's not empty because fish keep jumping up and taunting you.

Just because you didn't get any bites doesn't mean you didn't do things correctly. This makes it really difficult to follow the system you have been taught if you are new. A new person has no recollection of the times the system worked to fall back on when times are hard.

Ok, let's compare this with fishing again. Let's say that you are planning to go fishing for the first time and for some reason you decided to go alone.

You stop in the local bait shop to get bait and tips on what you should do. The shop owner tells you everything step by step and even shows you how to bait the hook. You look around the shop and the there are several pictures of the shop owner showing his successful days on the lake. Since he seems to really know what he is doing, you trust his directions and you follow them exactly.
You go to the exact spot he tells you to go to, and there is only one other person there (a lady). You stay out there for hours doing exactly what you were told, but you don't even get a nibble.

Finally, you are fed up, so you pack your things and leave. You then go back to the bait shop and you say to the owner, "You didn't know what you were talking about. That stuff doesn't work!". Then the lady that you saw at the lake walks in with a cooler full of fish.

You ask her where she got them and she says that she caught them at the lake where you saw her earlier. After talking to her and getting all of the details, you realize that she did the exact same things that you did, yet she caught many fish and you caught none. She then tells you that she went to the same spot on the same lake the day before and she didn't catch anything.

She did everything the exact same way and yesterday she caught nothing, but today she caught plenty. She then tells you that she has had **many** days that she caught absolutely nothing. While the lady no doubt has more experience than you, her experience and skill are not the primary reason for her success – It's her Self Development.

The biggest difference between you and the lady is that the lady believes in the system, and in taking the necessary time to not just get good, but to master the system. Many of you reading this didn't get your desired results the first time you attempted your business or your system, and you were ready to quit. **Self Development helps you to believe that if you continue to do the things you need to do, you will eventually get the desired results.** You don't quit or give up when things get rough. You continue to develop your skill and tweak some things, but never completely give up.

Another thing that Self Development does is it helps you get out of your own way. You must learn to eliminate the fear of making money, the fear of having money, and the responsibility that you think comes with running a business large enough to generate 5 figures a month.

Notice that I said the responsibility that you THINK comes with running a business that generates a lot of money. Don't get me wrong, there is definitely responsibility involved in running a business, but it usually is not as bad as it is imagined to be. Many people self sabotage due to the exaggerated expectation of responsibility. They literally stop people from signing up in their businesses. How you ask?

Some don't follow up.

Let's say that there is a business owner who has someone contact them (we will call this business owner Todd). Todd has someone who contacts him and says "Todd, I want to sign up on your business team this Friday when I get paid. Call me on Friday and I will sign up." Friday comes and Todd has not forgotten that he is supposed to call the prospect/potential team member, but he doesn't call because deep down he is afraid to be the person that someone else looks to for leadership.

Another way people self sabotage is by making excuses. Let me clarify that statement. When I say people self sabotage by making excuses, I don't only mean it in the typical way. I mean that they make excuses for other people. A better way to say it is that they *give* people excuses.

Let's again use Todd as an example. This time, someone calls Todd and actually gets him on the phone. Let's call this person 'TF' for Todd's friend (What can I say, I'm feeling creative). So TF calls Todd and says *"Hey Todd, I checked out your web link that was on your business card, and your business sounds awesome! I have my credit card here and I am ready to sign up. Can you help me?"*

Now this is many Network Marketer's dream come true, but some people are terrified to be in this situation.

Ok, so TF (Todd's friend) is ready to go, but then Todd says ..."*Well hold on TF, didn't you just put 4 new tires on your car?*" Then TF says "*Yeah Todd. I sure did. It cost me a pretty penny too!*" Then Todd replies "*Well, how about we just get you signed up next week? You already had to spend sooo much money!*" Then TF says "*Good thinking. Yeah, I can always get going next week.*" Does this sound familiar to anyone? Does this sound like you? (Don't forget that we agreed to be honest with each other.)

Lastly, we will discuss the people who are overconfident. Now this is not typical self sabotage because it is unintentional, but it still falls into the same category. These are the people who think they are immediately equipped with everything they need to fly to the top of their company's production list.

In other words they are know-it-alls. They don't listen. They don't do all of the things they should be doing, but they expect great results. Then as soon as things don't go as planned, they are ready to quit.

Self Development helps with all of this as well. Self Development is more than motivation or making you believe in yourself. It is also learning techniques and developing actual skill sets.

Let me give you my own personal Self Development testimonial. I was first introduced to Network Marketing at around age 16 and I started my first business at age 18. I went to company trainings and events but I didn't get much better initially. But over time, I started to notice a difference.

Let me be clear, not all training/self development is created equal. The trainings and instructions I got early on in my career weren't the greatest. Now don't get me wrong, they meant well and they were just telling us to do the things they were doing. The problem is although those things worked for them, they didn't work for everyone (We will get to why that is later).

The things that I was taught early on were basic and they just didn't work. Things like "don't waste your time talking to friends and family" were being taught by every Joe Blow on the internet trying to make a quick buck. Most "Industry Pros" and company trainings were telling you to say terrible lines like "Would you be open to a business opportunity?" (I think I just gagged a little).

Many of you might be doing or saying these things right now. If you are, I would wager that you aren't doing so well in your business. I used to wonder how some people were making money doing the things that we were taught. Truth be told, I got to the point where I wondered if the industry was even real. As I began to meet more and more people, I found out that many of the so called money makers were either broke or used underhanded tactics to get to their positions. I was ready to quit the industry, but quitting things is not in my nature, and I surely couldn't quit without making sure that I had given it my all.

Then I had a thought that changed the course of my life. I thought "If I was going to be a Dr. or a lawyer, I would be paying 100's of thousands to educate myself". Although I'd had lots of training, I had never taken my training seriously enough to pay money for it.

The problem was at that point, I was "broker" than I had ever been in my adult life. So it took almost all of the money I had, but I went to trainings by people who had real success in this industry by doing things the right way (Talking to people and building relationships).

Finding someone who could teach me how to do things the right way was much more difficult than it should have been. There were numerous people who tried to sell/teach internet marketing short cuts, but not very many who were actually talking to people.

Please don't misunderstand me. Internet marketing pertaining to Network Marketing can be a great tool to use to find new people to talk to, but **it does not take the place of actually talking to people and building relationships**. Again, the internet should be used to get new prospects to TALK to, not to replace talking to people all together.

Nothing outside of talking to people and building relationships works long term because that is the only thing that duplicates, and this is an industry of duplication. You can either take time to try to find another way, or you can spend that time getting great at building relationships and talking to people.

So don't fight it. You could possibly make money without learning to deal with people, but I have never seen anything else duplicate. Duplication is what makes your team grow without you having to have a hand in everything. This is where that "walk away" residual income comes from.

So, after I started real self development,

everything in the industry changed for me. I can't pinpoint the exact moment, but somewhere along the way, I got pretty good at this thing. Everything from the type of company I wanted to join to the way I talked to people was different.

I could really see the difference when I ran across someone who was trying to use those stale lines and tactics that I learned early in my career. I was a shy person, so I really didn't want to have to deal with people, but I knew that in order for me to get the nice things that I wanted out of life, I was going to have to get uncomfortable and learn to deal with people.

I have good news and bad news. The bad news is that I had to get uncomfortable in order to change, but the good news is that once I got serious, it didn't take very long. I don't know how much time it will take you to become a professional, but procrastinating only makes it take longer. Buckle down and go through whatever it is that you need to go through so that you can change your life. That change starts with facing your fears. Facing your fears starts with action. Overcoming those fears starts with taking action and Self Developing at the same time.

So buy some CD's or DVD's to listen to in your car. Download some programs on your phone. Are you low on funds? That is no excuse because there is so much free information available to you. Get a book from the library. Watch videos on You

Tube. Ask your enroller if he or she has some materials that you can borrow. Just don't make excuses. I don't make them, and I don't take them.

As humans, we have an ability to make ourselves believe things. If you hear something enough, you will eventually start to believe it. If you keep hearing that you are awesome and you can do anything, then it will eventually become your truth. So make yourself believe positive things instead of the negative lies that we tend to believe very easily. Repetition is the key to consistency and consistency is the key to change. Make self-development a constant in your life.

One of my favorite quotes is a very fitting way to end this chapter. *"When you say **'I can't**,' your brain says "ok". But when you say **'how can I?'**, your brain finds a way."~Author unknown.* So make sure that you are constantly developing yourself.

Strategies and Systems

We have covered why you need a coach and why you should self develop. Now it's time to get to some strategies...but before we do, let me give a disclaimer.

DISCLAIMER: If you jumped straight to this section and have been slacking on your actual Self Development like we discussed earlier, then this section won't matter for you. If you cut corners, lack confidence, are overly aggressive, or people simply don't like you, then strategies won't matter. So make sure that you are self developing.

Now that we have that out of the way, let's get to it. Your strategy, plan, system, or whatever you call it is very important. It is actually a very close 2nd to Self Development. A person at a high enough developmental level can possibly make money with no system. But a person who is underdeveloped is eventually going to fail, no matter what system they use. When your business out grows your development, your business is likely in trouble. It's only a matter of time if your development doesn't catch up.

To balance things out, don't feel like you have to be this super person before you start your business. If you don't own a business already, get the jump on your development now before you get one. But if you are already a business owner, do your development **while** you work your system.

Don't use your lack of Self Development as an excuse to do nothing.

WARNING: I am about to use a very cliché Network Marketing phrase....."Learn while you earn". Actually, I prefer the phrase "Earn while you learn" because the learning should be constant whether you are making money or not.

Guess what...you are going to make mistakes...Probably a few of them. But the good news is that while it is possible, it is highly unlikely that you will make a mistake so terrible that a high skill set can't fix it.

One of the biggest fears of many Network Marketers is that they will say something so terrible that it will change someone from a prospective business partner or customer to an eternal enemy.

Now don't get me wrong, you can definitely say things to get a person to tell you *"No"* (cliché alert) ,but **"No" really does mean "Not Right Now".** If you believe "No" actually means "No", then you are in for a rough road and your business days will be very short lived because most people are going to tell you "No" before they tell you "Yes".

I'm considered a pretty good "recruiter". This means that I am good at getting people to join my team as business owners. I earned a car, luggage, jewelry, and other things. But if memory serves me correctly, I had only 2 people who said yes to being a business owner the very first time I presented my (most successful) business opportunity to them. Believe it or not, most people aren't going to join *you* the first time either.

So if you have a problem with people telling you "No", you need to change your perspective on the issue. Instead of hoping you will only get "Yes", learn how to deal with the people who tell you "No". Again, "No" doesn't mean No, it means "Not Right Now".

To really understand this, you have to understand human nature. Even though it seems like it, human nature is not necessarily to *"say no all of the time"*. Actually it **(human nature) is** ***"not saying yes"* the first time.**

Many people feel like suckers if they say yes to spending any amount of money the first time an offer is presented to them by someone wanting to sell them something. If they go into a store where they can shop on their own, then they may quickly make purchases without thinking, but that is different. That is **their** decision.

When <u>you</u> approach them, they feel like they need to "think about it". This is why the art of *-making someone feel like what you want them to buy is their decision-* is so important to learn. You and I know that starting a home business is not as big a decision as many people make it out to be, but to the person making the decision it is huge! Maybe it was huge to you too. Your business probably cost you somewhere between $40 and $1000, and you very likely said "No" the first time you were presented with your opportunity. Even if you didn't say No, I would wager that you didn't say Yes the first time.

So again, my point is don't fight human nature. You will lose. Instead, embrace human nature and use it to your advantage. Ok, back to the systems.

It is possible to make money in Network Marketing without a good system. No, that was not a typo. You can make money without a good system. But odds are you didn't start your business just to make money. Most people start a business to gain freedom. Making money and having freedom both deal with money, but they are not exactly the same thing.

You could start a business, and make money by signing up new business partners and customers. That will definitely make you some money, but it won't make you free. If you stop signing new customers and business owners without a system or strategies, then the money will eventually stop, because everything depends on you. But when you have a good duplicable system, you can teach others how to do what you do. Remember, **people can learn a system, but they can never learn to be you**.

If you use a system to sign up new business partners and customers, you are equipping your team for success. So instead of you being the only one who can sign people up, you can have a team of people who not only know how to sign people up, but they also know how to teach the system to their new people and so on and so forth.

You doing it all yourself is just a "better sales job", but you plus a team of business partners all doing it together and teaching others to do it is freedom. If achieving this goal was easy, everyone would be doing it. Business isn't easy (especially initially), but with a great system in place, it can be simple. If someone tells you that business is easy starting out,... run away, don't walk. They are either naive or they are getting ready to take you for a ride. Now let's get more specific in regards to strategy.

STRATEGY:
THE WHAT AND THE WHY

When I started my Self Development, I went to people who were doing things the right way (talking to people and getting duplication) so that I could learn and develop the necessary skills to have some longevity in this industry. I knew I had to have duplication. I knew that I needed something completely different from the basic tactics that I had been taught earlier on in my career...you know, the tactics that don't work but sound really good.

What we are about to get into in the next few chapters will be very different from those basic tactics. Some of the things that we are about to go over might sound strange to you, but that's a good thing. If I were to tell you the same things that you have already been doing, then you would continue to get the same results, right? Let's get started.

We have talked a lot about duplication. The big problem in this industry is that once someone makes some money, people assume that this person can show them how to make money as well. That is a logical assumption, but being logical doesn't make something true.

Why wouldn't a successful person be able to show someone else how to do what they did? Let's make a scenario.

There is a man who is the Pastor of a church.

It's not a huge church, but he does have a Sunday congregation of about 400 people. Someone approaches him about a type of business he has never heard of before. It's called Network Marketing and it sounds awesome. So the person tells the Pastor that he (the Pastor) needs to get as many people as possible to a meeting and they will then get his people signed up.

Since the Pastor has a congregation, he makes an announcement one Sunday after service, and half of the people are interested. At the meeting, all of the people sign up.

When all of the Pastors commissions are totaled up, the pastor makes nearly $10,000 in his first week. The company of course notices the

Pastor's success, so they get behind him and hype him up as an example of what could be accomplished. They really hope that his quick success will motivate the other business owners in the company.

So they put him on all of the company promotional materials and he even gets to do some training on stage at the national event. Everyone wants to join the team of the man who made $10,000 in his first week.

It just so happens that the head of the city's school board (HSB) in his town was one of the people in the congregation who signed up that first week, and she knows even more people than the Pastor.

With the speed of his success and the company backing him, the Pastor is a bonafide star in the company now. The Head of the School Board (HSB) is using him as an example of their teams success and potential.

She spreads the word, and in 2 weeks she has signed up more people than the Pastor. She ends up making a little over $12,000 in one week.

So now the Pastor has a team of over 600 people (not even including his customers) and he finishes with a grand total of more than $50,000 in his first month!...and the company makes sure that everyone knows it.

Most people would assume that this is a well-oiled machine, but let's dig a little deeper.

Remember there are about 600 business people on his team. Let's assume that all 600 people followed the directions of their leaders exactly.

While 2 of the 600 were having great success, at the end of a 2 month period, only 10 people had made any money. That's 10 out of 600. So 590 out of 600 didn't make a dime. Do you still feel like this is a successful team? I didn't think so.

What would typically happen after that is many of those people would quit the business altogether. Let's say 300 of the 600 people quit after 2 months. Now that huge 600 person team is down to 300.

But the Pastor made so much money that his success continues to drive him. The HSB has just started to really tap into her market. So both the

Pastor and the HSB each add another 200 people bringing the Pastors team total to 700 people. So the team is still growing.

The Pastor and the HSB are so "successful" that they don't even have time to worry about the people who are falling off. I mean they can't focus on the struggling people, they have to focus on the new people who "really want it". So eventually the flames start to die out and the Pastor's personal signups begin to fall off. 6 months later, the Pastor's team is down from 700 to 200, and the HSB is down to 50 business people.

The Pastor has seen the writing on the wall. Since he was so popular, other companies heard of his success as well. One of those other companies offered the Pastor a $150,000 bonus to leave his current business and bring his team to their company.

The Pastor decides to take the offer and he moves to the new company, but he can't get nearly as many people to come with him since most of them didn't have any success the first time. Oh, and I forgot to mention that the Pastor was indeed paid a $150,000 bonus, but no it was not shared with the team. That bonus was for him.

Anyway, since things weren't going the way he wanted, he quit the 2nd business and vowed to never again own a Network Marketing business.

Ok. There is a major question that this scenario should cause you to ask.

Question: How is it that some people are so successful and others are not, when everyone is mimicking the same actions of the successful person? Why weren't the other team members successful if everyone is doing the same thing?

I am going to answer these questions with what in my opinion is the biggest reason some people are successful and others aren't, and you probably have never heard anyone talk about it as a reason for success...

THE MOST MISUNDERSTOOD FORCE

IN NETWORK MARKETING

Why were the Pastor and the HSB (Head of the School Board) so much more successful if everyone on the team was doing the same things? The difference is **Influence**.

Influence is a double-edged sword. It can be the best attribute a person on your team could have or its misapplication can cripple your whole team.

The Pastor from the previous chapter has a lot of influence. Influence can be great because people with influence tend to have more people in their network, and more importantly, they are better able to get people to take action since they have influence.

The downside of having influence is that it can make people lazy and cover bad habits and strategies. The absolute worst thing about influence as it pertains to Network Marketing is it can't be taught or duplicated.

Let's make a scale of influence with rankings of 1-5 with **1** being 'No one respects you enough to do what you ask' and 5 being 'Nearly everyone will do something simply because you do it'. You sometimes don't even have to ask them to do it.

Let's go back to our example scenario of The Pastor and The Head of The School Board (HSB). The Pastor and HSB are 5s on our influence scale. They have many people who will tell them "Yes", but those same people would tell most others "No". The only issue is that in my experience, the majority of people are **1**s or 2s on this scale, and like I mentioned earlier, influence can't be taught.

So let's say that a 5 on this scale signs up a **1**(a person with no influence). The **1** is very excited to be working with the 5, so the **1** immediately says *"Ok '5', I am ready to make money like you do! What do I need to do first?"*. These are some of the answers '5' might give you...

"-First, *Send your people to me and I will take care of them for you!"*- This can possibly work really well for you, if and only if, the 5 raises you up as a leader. Let's play this out.

So '**1**' gets a new prospective business partner

on the phone with '5'. Since '5' is so influential, it is not long before '5' has the new prospect eating out of his hand. The problem is that many people want the glory all for themselves, so they just leave you sitting on the phone like a flunky.

What '5' should do at the end of the call or meeting, is use his influence to build you up to the prospect, and if you are a 5, then you should be using your influence as the expert to build your team members up. That will help them to be able to run the business without you. Unless you have a huge ego, this should be what you want. There is no way your business can be self sustaining if the only person anyone will listen to is you.

Now let's talk about influence and the 3-way

call. The 3-way call should work like this… I get my prospect on the phone with my team member (the expert). Then I build my expert up as I introduce the two. Your prospect might feel like talking to you is nothing special, but they should feel like it is a privilege to talk to '5' (your expert). Why?

Because you built them up. Let me give you an example of a build up. –

"Hello Brother. I have '5' on the line with us. '5' is a Pastor with a huge heart for helping people, and he has helped a lot of people. He is not only brilliant, but he is a great person. He took time out of his schedule to talk to you today.

Pastor, this is my brother (<u>your brother's name</u>)."

It is very important to make sure that you are being honest about your expert when you introduce them, but that is (in general) the way this part of the conversation should go.

Please notice that I didn't build the prospect (brother) up at all. This was intentional. Remember, the person you build up is the person who has the power. So if you want the prospect to join your team, give the power to your expert.

At the end of the call, your expert should in turn give that power right back to you.

They (the expert) should end the call something like this.... *"And Prospect, I just want you to know that you have an awesome leader in '1'. You are very fortunate to be on her team, so make sure you really pay attention to what they ask you to do because she really knows her stuff!"*

Let me give you a real life example. I had someone do a 3-way call for me one time and my expert (my 5) initially didn't know what she was doing. Although I built her up initially, she never gave that power back to me. After the call, I had to tell her to build me up in the future, because what was happening was at the end of my calls, my prospects only had respect for her and not for me. Why? **Because I gave her the power and**

she didn't give any of it back.

I would ask my business partners to do something simple for their business and they would say *"Well what does she, (my expert 5) think about this?"* or *"Did she tell you to tell me that?"*

They thought that she was the only one who knew what she was doing. This is the problem with the " *Send everyone to me*" approach that many 5s will have you take.

Your prospects can turn into someone else's prospects if the person with influence is not willing to give that power back to you by endorsing you to *your* prospects.

Another negative thing a 5 could say to a **1**

when the **1** asks *"What do I need to do to start making money?"* is give them some cheesy line like *"Would you be open to a business opportunity?"*. I have heard variations of this line for years.

Only someone with great influence could get this line to work. Again, someone with influence can say pretty much anything and people will still sign up.

If a person with limited influence uses this line, it is likely going to fail most of the time. Why would it fail? Because the line is terrible!

What works best in business regardless of influence level is being natural. Talking like a regular human. Don't let a '5' fool you into thinking that lines like that will work for you.

Whether intentionally or not, the 5 usually makes the **1** feel like the **1** is doing something wrong because the magic words aren't working. '5' doesn't understand the power of influence any more than '**1**' does. '5' feels like..."The **1** must be doing something wrong because the line should be working!"

Now the **1** is frustrated because he is doing exactly as he is told, but it is not working. To make matters worse, he is being treated as though he is doing something wrong.

The truth is 5s have so much influence that it doesn't matter what they say because people want to join them regardless. When a person feels like you can help them accomplish their goals, it almost doesn't matter what you say because they have already decided that they want to work with you.

The only way a 5 could make those cheesy lines work for a **1** is if the 5 could teach the 1 how to have influence. Influence can't be taught, so what the 5 is doing does not duplicate. If a person has little to no influence, it doesn't mean that the person can't be successful, it just means that the **1** has a lot less room for error than a 5.

A person whose influence is **1** has to be close to perfect in her technique, or the fundamentals. A **1** needs to be better than a 5 in technique in order to have the success a 5 tends to experience.

Think of influence as "Talent" in sports. Let's use basketball for our example. Some people have natural talents that you can't teach, for example: running fast, jumping high, or just being tall. If a person is slow, can't jump, and short, then the only way they can compete is to be more fundamentally sound.

Tim Duncan, (a former professional basketball player) is tall, but (intelligence aside) that is his only exceptional ability. He is not the fastest runner, nor is he the highest jumper, yet he is considered by many to be the best power forward to ever play the game. While he definitely is not the most athletic player, he earned the nick name "The Big Fundamental".

He is great at the little things. The most unstoppable forces of all are the ones who are blessed with athletic ability and they are fundamentally sound. In Network Marketing, this is someone with influence who is also great at all of the fundamentals of our industry. If you are like most people and don't have much influence, you had better be great at following the system if you want to be able to compete. Then after you have some success, YOU will be the one with the influence.

WHAT DO I SAY? (OR NOT SAY) / USING TOOLS

This chapter is going to address what is probably the most popular question people ask once they start their business..."*What do I say?*"

Everyone is concerned with saying the right words. My experience has taught me that what you don't say is often more important than what you do say, and how you say it might be the most important thing of all.

One of the biggest problems for many people is that they talk too much. You should be using a system that consists of easily accessible (free or close to free) tools. Tools have a very important purpose; they allow duplication. Tools also do the talking so that you don't have to do as much talking yourself.

Remember, the best way to make sure that you don't talk yourself out of a sale is to not do much talking. If you are talking, you should be **asking questions** that will help you to better serve your prospects, not telling them why **you** think your opportunity is so great.

One of the main reasons I joined my last company is because they fully understood and implemented the same professional strategies that I had been taught when I decided to take my networking career seriously. I knew that their knowledge was going to make business easier for me than those companies that don't use professional strategies (which make things a lot more difficult for everyone). They had several great tools to help marketing reps present the business.

Let's talk about what good tools are, what they should include, and how you should use them. Most companies have the same types of tools, but the quality of the tools varies from company to company. A good introductory tool should as quickly as possible go over everything that the company has to offer. It doesn't matter if it is a website, a brochure, or a pre-recorded call. These tools should mention your main products, your business opportunity, and any other major aspects of your program. Your tools should then lead to your formal presentation (meeting, party, webinar, etc.)...if necessary. I say "If necessary" because sometimes you will show people your tools and they will want to sign up before they get to your formal presentation.

If this happens, then you get the sale done. (Don't lose a sale because someone told you initially that they wanted to sign up, but you wanted to push them through your whole process.) Don't forget your end goal.

Now if there is some important information that your prospect needs to know, then you need to be honest and share that information. No sale is worth damaging your reputation, but if the rest of your process does not consist of important information that could affect your prospects decision, then cut it off and sign them up if they are ready.

The reason all of your tools should include all aspects of your opportunity is two fold. The first reason is for you and your prospect. One of the biggest differences between a Network Marketing professional and someone who is incompetent is that incompetent people assume and pros don't. More specifically, **pros don't assume to know what aspect of their opportunity is of interest to the prospect.**

Wouldn't it be valuable to know exactly what aspects of your opportunity are the most important to talk to your specific prospect about?

You know how you find out? You ask them. This helps both you and the prospect. It helps you because it gives you valuable information about your prospect. It helps you to know what you should be talking to your prospect about.

It helps your prospect because they don't have to sit while you ramble on about something that they couldn't care less about.

The second reason all of your tools should touch on all that your company has to offer is because it gives your current and potential business partners options. Even if all tools are created equal as far as the information goes, people might still have preferences. You wouldn't want someone who is great at using the company magazine to be forced to use the company website simply because the website has more complete information. People should be able to use the type of tool that is the most effective for them.

Let's go back to reason #1. We talked about knowing specifically what you should be talking about to your prospect. Now we are going to go deeper into how you get that information. (I just want to let you know that this is one of the things that changed me from a rookie to a pro. So make sure that you pay attention to this section.)

When a tool makes mention of every aspect of the opportunity, your prospect is exposed to everything. After you present a tool, you ask the prospect the magic words that my mentor told me.... *__What did you like best__ about what you saw, heard, or read?"* The last part of that question of course depends on the tool you used. If someone looked at a magazine or a brochure, then you would ask *"What did you like best about what you read?"* If the tool was a video, you might ask

"What did you like best about what you saw?".

Let's compare this process to what a non-professional would do. Here is an example. Let's say that the 3 focal points of your presentation are money, product, and a free car. An amateur might start running off at the mouth trying to talk the prospect into the business, and they tell the prospect all of the things that they (the amateur) like. The amateur is excited about the free car you can earn.

I mean who doesn't want a free car?

I'll tell you who…a person who already has a car, and is broke, that's who. So the amateur goes on and on about something that doesn't interest the prospect at all.

If the business owner in our example was a professional, after the prospect finished the tool, he would have asked the prospect *"What did you like best about what you saw?"* As the old phrase goes, "Don't be a tool, use a tool". You are not a tool. You can't be duplicated by other people.... but information on a prerecorded call, a website, a magazine, or a DVD can be duplicated.

There are many aspects of a good process that you can put your own spin on, but "the question" is not one of those things.

Make a habit of asking *"What did you like best?"*

I have heard people change the question and say things like *"So what did you think about what you saw?"* This might seem like it's close enough, but it's not.

In fact, this is a terrible question. I am a firm believer that asking the right question will lead you to the right answer. You don't want to know what your prospect thinks, you want to know what it is that he/she **likes**.

Let's say that you did ask someone *"So what*

did you think about what you saw?". You might get an answer like *"Well, I thought the video was too long and that CEO was boring!"* That wasn't quite what you had in mind was it?

Sometimes you will get the wrong answer even when you ask the right question. Sometimes when you ask *"**What did you like best about what you saw?**"*, the prospect will say something like " *Well, I didn't like how that scientist talked."* Or they might try to ask you a question instead of answering your question.

You might say *"**What did you like best about what you heard?**"*, and the prospect might reply *"Well how much does it cost?"*. This is when you have to have strong posturing and get the prospect to give you the answer to your question because that information is vital to your success.

You can say something like this:

"We will definitely get to that. So what did you like best about what you heard?"

Notice I just repeated my question. Why did I repeat it? **Because they never answered it**. It is very important that you get this information, so you have to have strong posture. (If your posturing is weak, people will run over you).

You don't need to know what they didn't like, you need to know what they like. So, be firm (but polite) and find out what they liked. Don't be afraid to get the answer. After you get the answer, ask the question again. You know why? Because some people like more than one thing. I usually ask this question twice, three times max.

Knowing what to talk to someone about initially is one reason that the question is important, but there is another very important reason why you want to ask that question and find out what your prospect liked best. You need this information to find out the real reason they want to do business. This reason is known as their "Why".

THE FOLLOW UP

This is an extremely important section. There is an old industry saying "The fortune is in the follow up". You need to take that saying and make it a part of your life.

One thing you must understand is that most people aren't going to sign up the first time you present them with something that costs money. People usually need multiple exposures before they part with their hard earned money. This is why someone came up with the phrase "The Fortune is in the follow Up."

If you want to make a fortune, then you must be great at following up. I once read a sales study that said only 2% of people make purchases the first time something is presented to them. If this is accurate, then it means that it will be necessary to follow up with 98% of people! So you had better be great at it.

If you remember, in the previous chapter we talked about finding out a person's **'Why'**. We also said that there is a very important reason for that **'Why'**. The reason is that the Why is what makes your follow up effective.

Let's look at a situation that compares amateur follow up to professional follow up. This is actually going to be a pretty lopsided comparison since many amateurs don't follow up at all.

When someone tells an amateur "No", an

amateur believes it! They think "No" means "No" and they don't call back at all. Some amateurs know better than that, so they do check on prospects after they are initially rejected, but they just call back and say things like *"So, are you ready to get started?"*. This is definitely better than not calling at all, but it isn't likely to be very effective. Let's compare this to what a Pro does.

A Pro has already found out what the prospect likes and why they (the prospect) need whatever it is that you have to offer.

When you know the 'Why', you follow up with that 'Why'. This makes your follow up much stronger than if you followed up with a generic question like *"Are you ready to get started?"*.

I will use an example to show you how all of this works.

Let's say that there is a man who is introduced to a coffee business. The coffee has many special attributes including increased energy, tooth whitening, super strength, and lowering blood pressure.

Of course everyone wants to hear more about the super strength right? But when we asked this man what **he** likes best, we found out that he liked the fact that it whitens your teeth! His answer allowed us to find out his reason- **'Why'** he was interested in tooth whitening.

His 'Why' was due to the fact that his wife left him because his teeth were brown. He vowed to keep his teeth so white that that would never happen again! So instead of Following Up like an amateur and saying *"So, are you ready to order your coffee?"* you follow up like a pro and say " **Mike, I was just calling back to see how your tooth whitening is going. Have you found anything to give you that maximum whitening <u>so that you never again have to worry about someone leaving you for having brown teeth?</u>"**.

Which one of those do you think would be the most effective, the first or the second? Hopefully you are able to see the differences between what you might be doing and what you SHOULD be doing when dealing with your prospects.

We didn't just hit him with the generic

question, we hit him with something that would resonate with him emotionally. We hit him with not just a problem, but we hit him with **his** problem! I don't care who you are, if you have a problem, there is only so long that you can hear about the possibility of a solution to your problem and not take action.

If solving their problem really means something to the person, then it (the problem) will be crucial to your follow up process. This is why it is so crucial to go as deep as possible when trying to get someone's reason - their 'Why'. Your Follow Up won't be nearly as effective without it.

An ineffective Follow Up is a recipe for disaster in this industry because most people are not going to sign up the first time you present something to them. You will have to follow up with most of the people you talk to, so get GREAT, not good at figuring out what people like, then 'Why' they need what it is that they like, and finally, how to effectively follow up using that information.

Once you incorporate this into your system, you will see a significant change for the better in your business. Remember, it is often the little things that are keeping you from achieving your dreams when it comes to your business.

THE CLOSE

Many years ago when I first entered the Network Marketing business model, the whole idea of it changed my life forever. It changed my perception on how money could be made.

Even when I was working a job or a business in a different industry, NM still played a major role in how I did things. But as far as actually making money, things were much more difficult than they should have been. I was so hungry for knowledge, but I couldn't find anyone who could show ME how to be successful.

My early businesses had people who were coaches, Pastors, and teachers who were successful, but none of them seemed to know what to tell a 19 year old college student with no influence.

Hopefully this book is exactly what you need to help you to be successful. I did my best to make sure that this book was an actual guide that is full of the information I wished I had when I first started my business.

I can follow directions, but that doesn't mater if I don't have the proper knowledge. That is where I once was...hungry and giving it everything that I had, but I was missing the knowledge. While you will still make mistakes, you don't have to start from square one making the same mistakes I made early in my career.

But the other side of that coin is that you don't

have any excuses either. You have exactly what you need to know at your fingertips. The only thing left is for you to tailor this information to your specific company and products. Then just get great at running people through your process.

I think of it as a game. You are not going to beat me. I am going to control the conversation and I am going to keep you on the subject. I will get you to answer my questions, and I will do it all with humility and a smile. Knowing what to do, and then doing it is all it takes. The more you do it, the better you will get at it. Then you can show others how to do the same thing that you did.

Now you have what you need to be able to go out and accomplish whatever you would like to accomplish in this industry, and I am here to help you in any way that I can.

I appreciate you purchasing this book and would be happy to offer my continued support.

May God bless you

and your business.

THE END

****

FREE DOWNLOAD

Get your free copy of the
5 Network Marketing Success
Killers mini-book.
Go to the web address below…

NmRegister.ekjbooks.com

****

Personal Goal Setting and Your Why

This section is for you to write **your** "WHY". Why are you in business?

Who are you doing this for?

What do you want to accomplish?

Why do you want to accomplish whatever it is that you want to accomplish?

_____

_____

_____

_____

_____

"I Wish My Whole Team Had This Book!"

If you can see the immense advantage it would be for all of your team members to have this book, then I have a special program for you.

Contact EKJbooks and let us know that you would like distributor wholesale pricing for orders of 20 books or more.

Email: support@ekjbooks.com

Cover photo credit: Tim Gouw-Unsplash